C000142110

THE POWERSTOCK FESTIVAL
CIDER COOKBOOK

Published by Milton Mill Publishing, Milton Mill
West Milton, Bridport, Dorset DT6 3SN

First Published in 2013

Text copyright © The Powerstock Cider Festival 2013
Front cover illustration and b&w drawings © Alex Ogg 2013
Watercolours of apples © Liz Copas
Food photos and orchard photo © Steve Luck 2013
Photos on pages 16, 73 & 74 © Annabelle Jackman 2013

All rights reserved.
No part of this publication may be reproduced, stored in a
retrieval system or transmitted in any form or by any means,
electronic, mechanical, photocopying, recording or otherwise,
without the prior permission of the copyright owner

Printed and bound by Creeds Ltd,
Gore Cross Business Park, Bridport DT6 3UX
Recipe text typeset in Calibri

ISBN 978-0-9540570-2-2

A CIP catalogue record for this book
is available from the British Library

RECIPE FOR SUCCESS

A brief history of cider making in West Dorset

A life without cider or apples in Dorset, or anywhere else for that matter, would not be worth contemplating. Apples, orchards, cider presses, cider barrels and cider barns have been our constant companions for hundreds of years and they made life as an agricultural labourer not only bearable but a joy. It was a calculated escape from the drudgery of farm work to another world, a world tinged with blossom and the fragrance of summers long past, sweet juice and rosy lips.

Cider was a passport to another world after a hard day's work whether it be sheep shearing, scything a field of hay or barley, or even hoeing turnips. And in the long depressing months of winter, cider is best mulled to avert colds, ills of the spleen, melancholy, colic, kidney stones, scurvy and other unmentionable diseases caught on a night out in Bridport. Cider was the cure all and indeed a potent aid to survival both physically and psychologically.

In Dorset cider was first mentioned in 1291 in the accounts for Shaftesbury Abbey. So the nuns were on the cider over 700 years ago!

No wonder the abbeys were dissolved. By 1340 tithes were being paid in cider in Beaminster: thirsty vicars. And by 1685 the intrepid horsewoman Celia Fiennes comments upon visiting one of her relatives in Netherbury, Mr Newberry: 'good gardens and orchards, much good fruite but all in a most rude confused manner.' What has changed! More interestingly he also has a *stillitory* for experimenting with distilling and making cider brandy. 'My distillations inform me… etc'

Mr Newberry or John Newburgh Esq FRS, as he is sometimes called, commented at length on Dorset cider in his letter to the Royal Society in 1664: 'The best cider fruit with us in this part of Dorsetshire (lying neer to Bridport) next to Pippin and Pearmain is a *bitter sweet* or as we vulgarly call them *bitter scale*.' Newburgh also comments on the size of the presses in East Devon: 'In Devonshire where their *wrings* (i.e. cheeses) are so hugely great that a hogshead or two runs out commonly, before the apples suffer and considerable pressure.'

As to the scale of orcharding it was vast and in 1812 Dorset was reckoned to have 10,000 acres. One tree alone in Powerstock was said to yield seven hogshead in one season, which is nearly 450 gallons.

So in West Dorset the tradition of cider and cider making was endemic. It is long, broad, deep and unbroken, and was kept alive by a small band of small farmers and those who ran secret underground cider clubs, whose membership was akin to the Mafia.

Today as can be seen at the Powerstock Cider Festival, cider is booming and a sure sign of a slightly anarchic, hillbilly, independent nonconformity which assures not only the future of cider and orchards but the identity and pride of an area reeking of local distinctiveness and diversity. There are as many tastes and flavours as there are cider makers, and the standard of cider making, as can be seen by the entries into local cider competitions, is very high indeed. A remarkable turnabout in less than 20 years. Some, near Shaftesbury, are even making perry.

Cider is therefore not only alive and kicking, but there has also been a distinct sea change in the perception of cider. A whole new generation are now drinking local cider (responsibly I hope) and many of these new cider drinkers are discerning young women who support the local food movement. Also at long last there are now some very fine women cider makers. What could be better than drinking the fermented juice from the Fruit of Paradise. I reckon it was a cider apple that Eve was holding in her hand.

As to the food and cooking with apples, these are second nature to anyone associated with cider and orchards, and in West Dorset many of the apples were dual purpose, i.e. they could be used for cider or for cooking. Farmers' wives knew full well what to do with them…

What impresses me about this recipe book is its sheer range and diversity. Cider will go with just about anything. The old recipes keep cropping up like syllabub which is akin to possett and is recorded in Elizabethan recipe books. Cider helps to makes fine soups and adds just that extra bit of depth and flavour. I personally use cider apples when making a red cabbage stir fry and have been known to fry sliced rings of cider apples up for breakfast in bacon fat to go with the eggs, bacon and mushroom. Also cider is very good in risottos and of course goes with chicken and pork, but is often left off the menu where fish is concerned, and I am very glad to see several fish recipes there. Strong fish like mackerel, gurnard and sea bass I always feel would go well with a good strong tannin cider, or even a bottle fermented sparkling cider.

This is a fantastic recipe book and I commend it to you wholeheartedly.

James Crowden

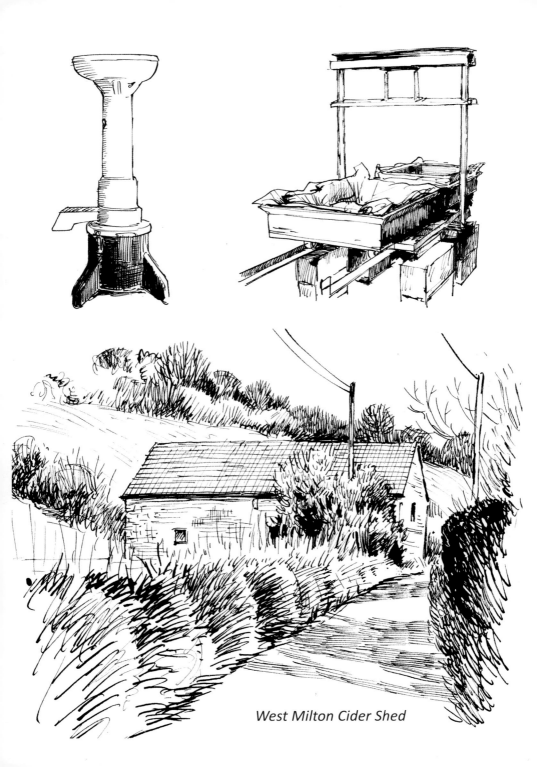

West Milton Cider Shed

DRINK UP THY ZIDER

Dorset has many faces. There is Purbeck Dorset, Hardy's Dorset, and the downland Dorset of chalk hills and cornfields. But none compare to West Dorset; different from all the rest, more like a stand-alone county in its own right, with Bridport as its capital.

Apart from the Devon border it has no hard-and-fast boundaries; only the crumbling cliffs of the Jurassic Coast, thick with fossils from Lyme Regis to Abbotsbury. Inland it melts away somewhere north of Beaminster, and Powerstock lies at the heart of it.

This is the Magic Circle: a rumpled, tumbling green-gold parish of plum-pudding hills and tangled valleys in which cider apple orchards have blossomed for generations.

Powerstock itself has a Norman church, a Saxon castle mound and a Victorian pub (The Three Horseshoes) that looks down on a thriving *Cider with Rosie* village school. To the west, just a mile down the dreamy valley of the little River Mangerton, lies the village of West Milton; and in the other direction looms Eggardon, the great Iron Age hillfort whose grassy ramparts dominate the eastern skyline.

Eggardon is not only a stunning viewpoint from which you can see the whole of West Dorset spread out at your feet, it's also a geological frontier - the last hurrah of the downland chalk - where the South Country ends and the West Country begins.

To find countryside half as good as this you'd have to travel at least as far as Normandy, whose lush green fields and apple blossom valleys bear an uncanny resemblance to our own West Dorset ciderlands. No surprise, then, to learn that it was probably the Norman monks of Loders who introduced the art of cider making to West Dorset, where it has survived to this day.

By the 14th century cider had overtaken ale as the common man's drink. The 17th century was its golden age and even in Thomas Hardy's day, cider was given to farm labourers as part of their wages. At haymaking, a labourer might put away two gallons a day – though how he still managed to work is a mystery.

When I first came to live in Dorset half a century ago the orchards around Powerstock had long since fallen into neglect. Cider making was fast becoming a lost art and the village press lay mouldering under its corrugated roof among the last greybeard trees.

But over the last couple of decades West Dorset has witnessed an extraordinary renaissance as part of the slow food movement espoused by the likes of Julian Temperley, the celebrated cider-maker who presides over a sea of orchards at Burrow Hill in neighbouring Somerset.

Temperley is a passionate advocate of what the French call *produits de terroir* – local produce. This is the antithesis of fast food, relying instead on local artisan products rather than supermarkets and mass production. Today, boosted by celebrity chefs such as Hugh Fearnley-Whittingstall, Lesley Waters and others, West Dorset is at the forefront of the slow food revolution and the growing interest in real cider is a part of it.

In *Dorset Up Along and Down Along*, a collection of reminiscences gathered by members of Women's Institutes, there is a fascinating description of how cider was made in the old days, when the apples were pressed with straw and reeds and the old men of the village sat around in their smocks, drinking from a tin mug used as a loving cup as they discussed village 'consarns'.

The West Milton Cider Club was founded in 2000 by Nick Poole and a group of local enthusiasts who meet once a month to chew over village 'consarns' just like our forebears - although nowadays it is denims instead of smocks and pint glasses instead of a loving cup.

Nick Poole it was who also founded the annual Powerstock Cider Festival in 2001, based on a successful tasting evening at the West Milton cider shed. Nick thought it might be interesting to expand the idea and hold it at Powerstock Hut. Right from the outset it was a huge success and over the years has had considerable influence over the resurgence of cider drinking and production in Dorset.

In 2006 this achievement was recognised by the Royal Bath and West Show who presented the Festival with their prestigious Award for Innovation.

The Cider Cook Book is Powerstock Cider Festival's latest venture in helping to promote the excellent local produce for which this unique corner of England is justly renowned and to encourage the use of real farmhouse cider in kitchens up and down the land.

Brian Jackman

CONTENTS

CIDER, LEEK AND PARSNIP SOUP

Oliver and Penny Strong, Dorset Nectar, Waytown

*This hearty winter soup is nectar indeed combining honest kitchen garden
vegetables with a generous helping of cider and cream.*

2 large parsnips
2 medium potatoes
2 medium leeks
*Reserve ½ cup green leek
  slices for garnishing*
800ml chicken stock
500ml artisan cider
225ml of whipping cream
½ tsp salt
dash of white pepper

Slice leeks, parsnips and potatoes and place in
pot together with the artisan cider and chicken
stock.
Cook about 30 minutes or until tender.
Strain and reserve the liquid. Purée the
vegetables until smooth, slowly adding the
liquid.
Add the cream and salt and pepper to taste.
Serve hot or chilled.
Garnish with thinly sliced green leek.

Serves 6

APPLE, ONION AND CIDER SOUP

Ian Skinner, Symondsbury

*Ian Skinner created this recipe for Pauline Bale of Highway Farm
for charitable fundraising events.*

75g butter
1kg onions, peeled and sliced.
2 large leeks, washed and sliced.
2 eating apples, peeled and sliced.
2 large potatoes, peeled and diced.
150ml cider.
1 litre veg or chicken stock.
3 bay leaves.
1 sprig of thyme.
200g gruyère cheese, grated.
2 heaped tbsp chopped chives.
grated nutmeg to taste.
sea salt flakes.
fresh black pepper.

Serves 6

Melt the butter in a large pan. Add the onions, leeks and apples and sweat until translucent (10-15 minutes).

Keep stirring regularly so the leeks and the onions don't brown. A brown onion is an unhappy onion, especially in a white soup. Add potatoes and stir.

Pour in the cider, bring to the boil and boil for a couple of minutes to reduce the liquid. Add the stock, bay leaves, seasoning, and thyme. Cover and simmer for 25 minutes until all the vegetables are cooked. Remove thyme and bay leaves. Blitz half the soup in a blender until smooth and return to the lumpy broth in the pan - this will give you that lovely texture.

To serve, ladle the soup into bowls and add a handful of cheese, some chopped chives and a pinch of nutmeg to taste.

Enjoy.

HOOKE SPRING FARM TROUT GRAVADLAX

Karl Bashford, The Three Horseshoes, Powerstock

A cider brandy and beetroot cure. It works equally well with other
oily fish such as salmon or mackerel.

1kg trout fillets
  (trimmed, pin boned, washed)
100ml cider brandy
1 bunch fresh dill roughly chopped
100g sea salt
50g caster sugar
juice of 1 lemon
2 raw beetroot
2 tablespoons crushed
  white peppercorns

Serves 6

Lay the fillets in twos on a triple layer of cling film ensuring there is enough film to wrap the fish several times.

Mix together the sugar and salt and rub into the flesh of the fish.

Blitz the beetroot in a food processor to make a purée.

Mix in the cider brandy and lemon juice, peppercorns and the dill.

Pour evenly over the fillets.

Now sandwich the fillets together in twos and wrap tightly in clingfilm.

Place fillets on a tray. A deep tray is needed as the fish will lose a lot of moisture and the beetroot will bleed out.

Place a slightly smaller tray on top, add a fairly heavy weight and put fish in the fridge.

Leave for four days turning fish every day and draining any liquid from the tray.

After four days wash the fillets under cold running water and dry.

Slice as thin as possible and serve with watercress, caper berries, horseradish & soda bread.

MUSSELS 'SAUCE CAUCHOISE'

Big Ben Restaurant, Fecamps, Normandy

1kg mussels
1 onion
1 apple (sliced)
150g lardons (bacon)
1 tbsp flour
1 glass of cider (medium)
pepper
5 tbsp fresh cream

Brush the mussels and wash them well under running water.

Slice the onion. Fry with lardons and apple for one minute.

Sprinkle in flour, stirring well. Pour in cider. Bring to the boil.

Add the mussels and simmer for five minutes, mixing regularly with the sauce.

Discard any shells that don't open after cooking.

Add cream and pepper to taste, stir and serve.

Serves 6

DUCK PARFAIT WITH CIDER JELLY

Karl Bashford, The Three Horseshoes, Powerstock

Parfait
500g duck livers
2 eggs
250ml double cream
Fine sea salt

Reduction
150ml cider brandy
3 cloves
1 star anise
3 juniper berries
2 bay leaf
1 diced shallot
whole clove of garlic

Jelly
300ml good cider
300ml good apple juice
50g caster sugar
4 leaves gelatine

Garnish
150g hazelnuts
baby cress

Serves 6

Blitz livers in a processor. Whilst motor is still running add the eggs and cream and season. Leave running until as smooth as possible. Place all the reduction ingredients in a pan and reduce by two thirds. Leave to cool for one hour to let flavours infuse.

Now strain the reduction into the liver mix. Pass the liver mix through the finest sieve or preferably a chinois. This will take time but is crucial as the smoother the mix the smoother the parfait will finish.

Transfer to six preserving jars. Cover with foil and place in a deep tray. Pour hot water into the tray until it comes half-way up the jars. Place in an oven at 180°C and cook for 10 mins. Continue to cook and keep checking every 10 minutes until the parfait is just set to a firm wobble. Remove from the bain marie, cool then refrigerate overnight.

Soak gelatine leaves in cold water until soft. Bring cider, apple juice and sugar to boil. Whisk in gelatine until dissolved. Strain and cool but be careful not to let set. When cool carefully pour jelly into jars to completely cover the parfait. Return to the fridge for two hours to set. Quickly roast hazelnuts in a hot dry frying pan. When coloured all over roughly blitz in a food processor although not to a powder.

Remove parfait from fridge, add some crushed nuts on top of the jelly and garnish with some baby cress. Serve with crusty bread

FISH STEW

Arthur Watson, Riverside Restaurant, West Bay

2 tsp butter
1 large leek thinly sliced
2 shallots finely chopped
125ml dry cider
300ml fish stock
250g potatoes diced
1 bay leaf
4 tbsp plain flour
200ml milk
200ml double cream
55g fresh sorrel leaves
350g skinless monkfish or cod fillet
 cut into 2.5cm pieces
salt and pepper

Serves 6

In a large saucepan melt the butter over a medium low heat.
Add the leeks and shallots: cook for five minutes stirring regularly.
Pour in the cider and bring to the boil.
Pour in the stock whilst stirring and then add potatoes, bay leaf and a large pinch of salt (if stock is not salty).
Bring back to the boil and then turn down the heat; cover and cook for ten mins over a low heat.
Take the flour and put into a small bowl. Slowly whisk in a few tablespoons of milk to create a thick paste. Stir in a bit more to create a smooth liquid.
Reduce the heat so that the stew is just simmering and then stir in the flour mixture.
Cook for another five minutes stirring regularly.
Pour in the leftover milk and half of the cream.
Cook for a further 10 minutes.
Chop the sorrel finely and mix into the leftover cream.
Pour the sorrel cream into the stew while stirring and then the fish.
Carry on cooking for another three minutes stirring now and again.
Season to taste and then serve.

SOLE IN CIDER

Arthur Watson, Riverside Restaurant, West Bay

60g butter
1 onion thinly sliced
1 garlic clove
80g smoked pancetta cubed
1 tbsp plain flour
375ml cider
1 bay leaf
8 sole fillets skinned
1 egg yolk lightly beaten
3 tbsp double cream
salt and pepper
fried bread to serve

Serves 4

Melt the butter in a pan, add the onion, garlic and pancetta and cook over low heat, stirring occasionally for five minutes
Sprinkle with the flour and cook, stirring, for a few minutes more
Pour in the cider, season with salt and pepper, add the bay leaf, increase the heat to medium and cook for 15 minutes until reduced.
Lower the heat, place the sole fillets in the pan and simmer gently for seven to eight minutes. Transfer the sole to a warm serving dish.
Remove and discard the garlic and bay leaf. Stir the egg yolk mixed with the cream into the pan juices, heat through for a few minutes, (do not allow it to boil) then pour the sauce over the fish.
Serve with thick slices of bread fried in butter.

FISH IN CIDER BATTER

Arthur Watson, Riverside Restaurant, West Bay

1 cup of plain flour
1 tbsp light oil
1 cup of ice cold cider
1 large egg
pinch of salt

Mix flour, salt and oil in bowl.
Beat in egg and ice cold cider
Coat fish with mix
Lower fish slowly into deep oil at 180ºC
Crisp and golden fish ready to enjoy.

POACHED SALMON IN CYDER

Sandie and Oxford Tom, The Marches Cyder Circle

2 salmon fillets
10g butter
2 bay leaves
100ml full juice real cyder (dry)
1 or 2 red chillies seeded and sliced
(you can leave the seeds if you like
it 'hot')

Serves 2

Pre-heat the oven to 170˚C .

Take enough silver foil to make a parcel to hold the fillets. Place in a small roasting tin.

Butter the centre of the foil and place the salmon fillets onto it. Put one bay leaf under each fillet and sprinkle over the sliced chillies. Finally spoon over the cyder and seal the parcel well top and sides.

Put in the pre-warmed oven and cook for 15 minutes.

Remove from oven and carefully open the parcel. Remove the bay leaves but leave the chillies (if wanted).

Serve with rice or new potatoes.

TROUT IN CIDER WITH FENNEL AND GINGER

Nick Poole, West Milton Cider Company

Poaching the trout in cider brings out the real sweetness of the fennel and ginger, and gives great balance to the trout. It's the type of recipe that allows you to adjust the final flavour at the end. Goes perfectly with a well chilled medium sweet cider.

2 medium sized trout
2 small fennel bulbs or 1 large, trimmed with the greenery saved.
15g of fresh ginger cut into matchsticks (julienne)
25g butter
1 tbsp olive oil
300ml medium sweet cider
powdered ginger to taste
50ml double cream

Serves 2

Start by heating the butter and olive oil in a frying pan big enough to accommodate the trout.

Cut the fennel bulbs into two, or four if you have a larger bulb - you are aiming for two good pieces per person. Add to the hot butter, cut side down, and cook until the underside is browning and beginning to caramelise. Turn over and continue cooking, adding the fresh ginger. When the fennel is nicely browned and reasonably tender add the cider.

Boil for two minutes then place the trout in the pan with the fennel. Cook the fish for about six to eight minutes per side depending, on the thickness. When ready (try not to overcook) remove the fish to plates and keep warm.

Now reduce the remaining cider sauce leaving the fennel in the pan (it should now be very tender and starting to fall apart).

At this stage the dish can be pepped up with addition of some powdered ginger, but taste as you add it.

When the cider has reduced to a suitable consistency, stir in the cream, and heat for a few seconds.

Place the fennel bulbs beside the trout on the serving plates and pour over the sauce ensuring all the gingery bits are added.

Garnish with a few green sprigs taken from the fennel bulbs before starting.

COD IN CIDER

Marie-Anne & Michel Ameline, Normandy

*This would normally be made with a French cidre bouché so try it with a
British sparkling cider or any medium cider.*

800g thick cod fillet
500g mushrooms
1 onion
5 shallots
1 clove garlic
2 tbsp olive oil
5 tbsp fresh cream
2 glasses cider (medium)
salt and pepper to taste
chopped parsley

4 big crisp eating apples
a little butter
1 glass cider (medium)
1 tsp ground cinnamon
1 tbsp brown sugar

Serves 6

Peel and slice the onion and shallots. Fry them in
half the olive oil until golden.
Wash and slice the mushrooms.
Add them to the onion & shallots and cook for
about five minutes.
Add the crushed garlic.
Lay the mixture in an ovenproof dish.
Fry cod fillets in rest of oil until brown. Five
minutes on one side only
Lay the fish on top of the mushrooms.
Pour the two glasses of cider into the pan; bring
gently to the boil, reduce heat and simmer until
the sauce gets a bit thicker.
Add the cream, mix well and turn off the heat.
Pour onto the fish. Cover with foil and bake for
20 minutes at 180°C.
Wash and cut apples in quarters without peeling
them. Fry gently in butter until golden. Turn
them over, sprinkle with cinnamon and sugar.
Add cider. Cook until they are soft and the cider
is absorbed.
Sprinkle fish with parsley and serve with apples.

CHICKEN IN CIDER AND CHEESE

Nick Poole, West Milton Cider Company

The perfect marriage of cider and cheese combine in this rich, full flavoured dish containing all the vegetables you need for a complete meal. It's great for dinner parties and events when you don't want to be spending ages in the kitchen with lots of different bits to prepare at the last minute. It can also stand being cooked in advance and reheated when required.

30g butter
2 tbsp oil
1 large chicken divided into
  eight portions
1 medium sized celeriac
2 leeks, white part only,
  sliced in 12mm lengths
2 sticks of celery
  sliced in 25mm lengths
300ml dry cider
200ml double cream
2 tbsp Dijon mustard
1 tbsp finely chopped or
  grated ginger
Pinches of nutmeg and
  cayenne pepper
175g mature Cheddar cheese
3 tbsp fresh bread crumbs

Serves 4

Heat half the butter and one tablespoon of oil in a frying pan and cook the chicken pieces for about fifteen minutes or until nicely browned all over. It is best to start with the skin side down. Transfer them to a small roasting tin or low sided casserole. Season with salt and pepper.
While the chicken is browning prepare the celeriac into 25mm dice and part cook in salted water for about seven or eight minutes. Using the remaining oil and butter, fry off the leeks and celery for about five minutes. Add all the vegetables to the chicken. Now add the cider to the frying pan and boil for two minutes scraping up any residual bits and left behind juices. Remove from the heat and allow to cool slightly then add the cream, mustard, ginger, two-thirds of the cheese and the spices.
Pour over the chicken and vegetables and sprinkle the breadcrumbs mixed with the remaining cheese. Cover with foil or a lid and bake in the oven for 20 minutes. Remove the cover and continue cooking for another 20-25 minutes until the top is nicely browned and the chicken fully cooked.

CHICKEN IN CIDER

Neil Worley, Worley's Cider, Shepton Mallett

This is a simple, thrifty meal using chicken legs and a good artisan cider. You will end up with chicken that's crispy on the outside but soft and tender underneath. There is also a rich cider and mushroom sauce to go with it. Not quite a one-pot affair, but it gets close!

4 large chicken legs (or 8 thighs)
1 pack chestnut mushrooms (any kind, but chestnut are tasty and not too watery)
400ml cider (medium)
knob of butter
bay leaf
2 sprigs thyme
double cream or cornflour (optional)
chopped parsley
English mustard

Serves 4

Season the chicken with plenty of salt and pepper and brown on both sides in a frying pan. Put chicken in a shallow, ovenproof dish.

Pour about half the cider into the frying pan and let it bubble while scraping the crispy chickeny bits off the bottom. Add to the dish and top up with the rest of the cider until it reaches about half way up the chicken. (This depends on the size of your dish really, so use your discretion.)

Chop mushrooms into chunky slices and fry in a generous knob of butter till the juices run and the mushrooms brown slightly. Tip into the dish with the chicken.

Tuck in the bay and the thyme.

Cook at 140°C for one and a half hours. The skin will crisp if you just leave it and don't baste or turn the chicken.

It is ready to serve like this if you want a broth-like sauce. Adjust seasoning and sprinkle with chopped parsley. A bowl of plain rice would be perfect to accompany.

For a more sumptuous dish, pour off the sauce into a pan. Whisk in a few tablespoons of double cream and a teaspoon of English mustard. Adjust seasoning, and add more mustard if required.

To avoid the cream, mix a few teaspoons of cornflour with some cold cider or water in a teacup. Add till you get your required thickness. Serve with mash and veg and a drop of cider to wash it down.

WINTER CHICKEN CASSEROLE

Penny and Oliver Strong, Dorset Nectar, Waytown

3 large onions – chopped
2 cloves garlic
small chilli (optional)
8 chicken thighs
250g fresh mushrooms sliced
2 leeks
1 tsp thyme
1 tsp sage
3 tbsp flour
6 parsnips thinly sliced
3 large potatoes, thinly sliced
salt and pepper to taste
400ml chicken or vegetable
  bouillon
400ml cider
2 spring onions for garnish

Preheat oven to 180°C.

In a large pan, sauté the onions, garlic and chilli in a little oil and butter till golden. Spread on the base of a large casserole or baking dish. In the same pan, now sauté the chicken pieces until brown, about 10 minutes. Remove the chicken and place on the bed of onions. Sauté the mushrooms, leeks and herbs then stir in the flour. Spoon the mixture over the chicken. Arrange the thinly sliced parsnips in the baking dish. Then arrange the thinly sliced potatoes on top. Pour over the bouillon and the artisan cider and place in the oven. Salt and pepper to taste. Bake uncovered in 180°C oven for 1 hour 20 minutes.

Garnish with spring onion slices and serve with a green salad

Serves 6

CHICKEN CIDER CURRY

Steve Brady, Marquis of Lorne, Nettlecombe

2 tbsp olive oil
4 chicken legs skinless & boned
1 clove garlic chopped
1 chopped onion
1 peeled, cored & chopped apple
1 tsp cumin
1 tsp coriander
1 tsp turmeric
150ml dry cider
2 tbsp sultanas
1 lemon
salt & pepper to taste
whipping/double cream
fresh coriander
  (keep some back for garnish)

Heat oil in a heavy-based frying pan. Fry chicken legs until coloured on all sides then add chopped onion and garlic. Continue to fry for two to three minutes.

Add cumin, coriander and turmeric. Stir well adding dry cider and then chopped apples, sultanas and chopped coriander.

Add cream. Continue to cook over a low heat for approximately 30 minutes.

Add a good queeze of lemon juice.

Taste to check seasoning and consistency and adjust if required.

Serve on basmati rice, sprinkled with chopped coriander. Accompany with poppadums, chutneys, pickles and naan bread.

Serves 4

LEFTOVERS CHICKEN PIE

Mark Rogers, Rogers' Cyder, Melplash

What do you do with the leftovers? Mark Rogers comes up with a brilliant suggestion that you'll want to make again and again.

2 small onions
chicken
1 tsp smoked paprika
  (chilli or herbs if preferred)
mix of veg eg, carrots, leeks, peas
  broccoli - anything left over but
  not enough for a meal
1½ tbsp flour
milk or cream

Pastry
300g flour (mix of plain and
wholemeal)
150g butter
up to 4 tbsp water

Serves 4 depending on the
size of the pie dish!

Roughly chop two small onions. Sweat them down until they start to caramelise. Deglaze the pan with a good slosh of cider.

Chop up some chicken or use the leftovers from a roast stripped off the carcass. Sprinkle with smoked paprika. Brown the chicken in the pan but don't dry it out! Keep feeding the pan with cider to stop it sticking and to build up a base for your sauce. It should be on a fairly low heat. While this is going on steam some other vegetables. Remove the chicken and add flour and, using a whisk, start to stir it together. Now pour in a little milk or cream - you are looking for enough sauce to combine the other ingredients but not enough to engulf them.

Turn the oven on and set it to 180°C

Rub in the flour with the butter until you have bread crumbs and then add enough water to bring it all together.

Roll out the pastry and line the dish, prick the bottom of the base to let the air out and bake in the oven until golden (about 20 mins). Roll out enough for the top.

Once the base is cooked, (golden but not brown) carefully load up the pie and put your top on. Brush milk over the pastry and seal the edges. It will need about 20 - 30 minutes to cook through and brown the top off.

Eat it with the rest of the cider and serve with cabbage or mash and peas.

MARCHER PHEASANT IN CYDER

Cheshire Matt & Lou, The Marches Cyder Circle

This is a simple dish of pesto-stuffed pheasant breast in a cyder and cream sauce.

30g butter
4 large fresh pheasant
breast fillets
8 rashers of streaky bacon
or pancetta
4 tsp of red or green pesto
(1 for each breast)
150ml of real cyder
100ml double cream
salt and ground black pepper
pine nuts to garnish

Serves 4

Make a slit in each of the fillets to make a pouch. Fill the pouch with a generous teaspoon of pesto.

Next, wrap each fillet with two rashers of bacon and place in a roasting dish.

Pour in the cyder and put a lid on the dish or cover with foil.

Place in a pre-heated oven at 200°C for about 30 minutes

Next, pour off the juices into a pan, while keeping the fillets warm in a separate dish. Bring the juices to the boil and reduce by a third. Turn down the heat and stir in the cream. Season with salt and pepper to taste.

Place the pheasant fillets on warm plates and pour over the creamy sauce.

Sprinkle with pine nuts and a little more ground black pepper.

PHEASANT WITH SOMERSET CIDER BRANDY AND APPLES

Julian Temperley, Somerset Cider Brandy & Burrow Hill Cider

50g butter
4 small pheasants
5 cox apples (or other firm
 dessert apples), peeled, cored
 and chopped
75ml Somerset Cider Brandy
425ml dry cider
125-175ml double cream
50g raisins soaked in
 4 tbsp Cider Brandy

Serves 4-8

Melt the butter in a large, heavy-based flameproof casserole over a medium heat. Add the pheasants and apples and gently cook until they are both browned. Remove the apples and set aside. Now, add one tablespoon of Somerset Cider Brandy to the pan and carefully ignite it using a long match. Once the flame disappears, return the apples to the pan, pour in the cider and bring to the boil. Reduce the heat, cover the casserole and simmer for 30 minutes, or until the meat is tender. Remove the pheasants and apple from the pan and keep warm.
Bring the contents of the pan to the boil and cook steadily until reduced by two-thirds. Stir in the cream, the remaining cider brandy and soaked raisins into the cider sauce. Return the pheasant and apples to the pan to heat through. Serve straightaway.

SOMERSET PORK WITH CIDER AND APPLES

Matthew Bryant, Haselbury Plucknett

900g diced pork
500ml cider
3 cooking apples, chunked
  (no need to peel)
4 onions, chopped
12 rashers of smoked bacon,
  chopped
4 tbsp of cider vinegar
2 tbsp of fresh thyme
1 tsp of sage
2 tbsp of fresh flour

Fry the meat and put into a casserole pot.
Fry the onions and bacon.
Add the flour and stir, then the cider and vinegar.
Boil and pour over the meat.
Add the apple and herbs and stir.
Cook in the oven for one hour.

Serves 6

PORK AND RICE CIDER PARCELS

Penny Whatmoor, Owermoigne Cider Museum

1 pork chop
60g rice (uncooked)
30g frozen peas
½ small carrot, diced
½ small onion, diced
1 tsp mixed herbs
salt and pepper
120ml dry cider

Preheat oven to 180°C.

Place the pork chop and rice onto a large piece of cooking foil in a baking tray.

Turn up the edges of the foil to form a bowl.

Sprinkle the peas, carrot, onion and herbs over the chop and rice.

Pour over the cider.

Pull up the edges of the foil and seal it up (like you would a Cornish pasty).

Bake for one hour.

Open very carefully as the steam is very hot!

Serves 1

PORK AND APPLE MEATBALLS IN CIDER

Maya Pieris, Four Seasons Preserves, Askerswell

For the meatballs

500g of minced pork
a small slice of brown bread
  made into crumbs
small onion, finely chopped
  or grated
small dessert apple peeled and
  cored, finely chopped or grated
1 tsp dried sage,
a grating of nutmeg
a little lemon rind
salt & pepper

For the sauce

400g tin of tomatoes drained and
  the juice set aside
500ml of dry cider
1 onion
bay leaves
salt & pepper

Serves 6

Mix all the ingredients thoroughly together and leave covered in the fridge to firm up for a few hours or overnight.

With a spoon or your hands form into balls – the size and number is up to you!

Liquidise a tin of tomatoes with the cider. Fry a chopped onion in vegetable oil till softened, add the meatballs and brown lightly then pour in the tomato and cider liquid. Add a couple of bay leaves to the liquid for further flavour.

Turn the heat down and simmer adding more cider and/or tomato juice if needed.

Adjust seasoning to taste.

Serve with a mixture of mashed potato and apple puree and other seasonal veg!

SAUSAGE CASSEROLE WITH CIDER

Penny Whatmoor, Owermoigne Cider Museum

For a really hearty dinner add dumplings to the casserole halfway through cooking.

8 pork sausages
1 large onion, diced
1 medium carrot, sliced
1 medium parsnip, sliced
500ml dry cider
fresh or dried sage, thyme and
  rosemary
25g plain flour
200ml chicken or vegetable stock

Preheat oven to 200°C.
Fry the sausages in a little oil until browned, remove from the pan and set aside.
Fry the onion, parsnip and carrot for five minutes, then add the flour and cook for a further two minutes, stirring all the time.
Add the cider, stock and herbs and bring to the boil.
Bake in the oven for 40 minutes.
Serve with fresh crusty bread.

Serves 4

TARLINGTON MILL   MICHELIN   DABINETT   TREMLETTS BITTER

PORK, APPLE AND CIDER FAGGOTS

Torkard Ray & Gail, The Marches Cyder Circle

Try this traditional fare for a kitchen supper with family or friends

500g pork - use a cheaper cut such
  as shoulder or belly - trimmed
500g pigs liver
200g bacon - any cheaper cut will
  suffice - trimmed
2 apples - sharp dessert or dual
  purpose apples are best - peeled
  and cored
2 leeks, sliced
1 onion, sliced
2 garlic cloves
3 slices crustless white bread
1 egg
4 tbsp rolled oats
1 tsp dried sage
1 tsp ground bay leaves
salt and freshly ground black
pepper to taste
oil for frying
plain flour and cornflour
1 litre dry 100% juice real cyder

Serves 6

Gently fry the onion and leeks in a little oil until soft. Crush one of the garlic cloves and add to the leeks and onion for a further minute or two and then leave to cool.

Mince the pork, liver and bacon, and put into a large bowl. Mince the cooked leek, onion and garlic mixture. Coarsely grate the apples and add the breadcrumb and remaining crushed garlic clove. Add the herbs and seasoning and mix the ingredients together.

Mix in the egg along with four tablespoons of oats. Add more oats if necessary to get a firm consistency that holds its shape.

Pre-heat the oven to 180°C. Lightly grease a high-sided roasting tin.

Shape the faggot mix to form rough cubes (five to seven centimetres) and coat in plain flour. Fry the faggots lightly on all sides until golden-brown and transfer to the roasting tin and place in the oven for 20 minutes. Pour the cyder around the faggots. Cover with cooking foil and return to the oven for a further 30 - 40 minutes. When cooked, remove the faggots and keep warm. Scrape any cooking residue from the bottom of the roasting tin and pour the entire contents into a saucepan. Use a little cornflour to thicken the sauce and adjust the seasoning to taste. If desired, slightly sweeten the sauce with a little sugar.

Pour the sauce over the faggots and serve with mushy peas and chipped or mashed potatoes.

ORCHARD HONEY & APPLE SAUSAGE ROLLS

Goggin Jane, The Marches Cyder Circle

500g butchers sausage meat
fresh herbs – sage etc.
salt and pepper
1 apple chopped small
1 onion finely chopped
butter for frying
good dash of real cyder
honey for glazing
puff pastry

Pan fry the cut up apple and chopped onions in the butter for 10 minutes or so. Add the herbs, salt and pepper and a good dash of real cyder. Reduce the liquid. Drain, then add the apple and onion mixture to the sausage meat – mix well. Roll out the puff pastry and cut into rectangles. Add some of the sausage meat mixture into each rectangle, wet edge with water and seal each parcel. Glaze with a little melted honey. Place onto a greased cooking tray and cook in the middle of the oven at 180°C - 200°C for 15 - 25 minutes. Keep an eye on them!
Best served warm.

PORK 'N CIDER PIZZA

Billy Lintell, The Stable, Bull Hotel, Bridport

A delicious pizza using local pork that has been minced and marinated in garlic, olive oil & fresh sage that goes well with the sweetness of the caramelized apple brandy apples & roasted red onions.

A pre-rolled pizza base (12-14"), shop bought or make your own.

Tomato sauce (enough to cover not smother the dough)

3 large peeled & sliced
 field mushrooms
150g minced pork
1 clove garlic, peeled and chopped
3 fresh sage leaves, chopped
2 tbsp olive oil
1 medium red onion, sliced
2 braeburn apples, less ripe the
 better, peeled cored
 and cut into eighths
6 tbsp white sugar
2 tbsp butter
4 tbsp cider brandy
2 handfuls of grated mozzarella
Salt & pepper

Serves 2

Marinate the pork in a bowl with the chopped garlic, sage and olive oil, salt and pepper to taste. Mix well and leave for at least one hour. When ready to use roll into small balls.
While the pork is marinating caramelise the red onion: place in a small metal tray, add some olive oil, salt and pepper and roast in a pre-heated oven 200°C for approx 10 - 15 minutes until golden brown.
Now the apples. Melt the sugar in a heavy based frying pan until deep golden brown in colour, add the butter and stir. Once melted add the apples and toss in the caramel liquid. Do not attempt to taste the sauce as it will be extremely hot! Add the cider brandy and burn away the alcohol. Set aside and allow to cool.
Now assemble your pizza. Either use a pizza stone or greased baking sheet.
Roll out the dough. Add the tomato sauce, field mushrooms and roasted onions and dot the pork balls around the pizza. Finally add the caramelised apples and grated mozzarella. Season well and cook for approximately 10 minutes at 250°C until golden brown and crispy.

RABBIT CASSEROLE

John Baker, The Ropemakers, Bridport

*Once a staple food in Dorset, it is time rabbit came back into fashion
and this is just the ticket for a cold winter's evening.*

1 wild rabbit, skinned, gutted
 and jointed
125g smoked bacon pieces
 chopped roughly
1 tbsp olive oil
1 large onion, thickly sliced
2 medium carrots, cut into
 1 cm lengths on the diagonal
2 celery sticks, cut into
 1 cm lengths on the diagonal
2 bay leaves
2 tsp mixed herbs
1 litre dry cider
1 tbsp clear runny honey
250ml double cream
2 tbsp grainy mustard
salt and freshly ground black
pepper

Serves 4

Heat the olive oil in a large, heavy-based frying pan. Gently fry the bacon until lightly browned and the fat runs. Transfer to a casserole. Brown the rabbit joints in the same pan, in batches, and place in the casserole. Now sweat the onion in the same pan until soft and translucent. Add with the carrots, celery, bay leaves and mixed herbs to the casserole.

Tightly pack the ingredients, then pour over the cider. It should just cover the meat. Add the honey and season with salt and pepper.

Bring to a simmer and cook, covered, at a very low simmer, for about two hours, until the rabbit is completely tender.

Place the rabbit pieces on a plate and remove all of the meat from the bones (be very careful as some of the bones are quite small).

Strain the stock through a colander into a clean pan, and reserve the bits of veg and bacon.

Boil the strained stock hard until reduced to a scant 50ml (yes, really reduce the stock). Then whisk in cream and the grainy mustard and boil for a couple more minutes, until thick and glossy, scraping in all of the reduced stock including the sticky stuff on the sides of the pan.

Taste for seasoning and adjust with salt, pepper and more mustard as you see fit. Mix the rabbit, vegetables and bacon with the sauce and warm through thoroughly.

Serve with creamy mashed potatoes and seasonal vegetables.

CASSEROLED BEEF WITH MUSTARD & CAPERS

Nick Poole, West Milton Cider Company

This is a great combination of sharper flavours meeting a slightly sweeter cider, happily blending together in the rich juices of the slowly cooked beef.

1 tbsp oil
1 large chopped onion
shake of mixed herbs
1 large tbsp of Dijon mustard
2 tbsp of capers in brine – rinsed
800g of stewing or casserole beef.
500ml of medium cider
120g pearl barley

Serves 4

Fry the onion in a heavy based frying pan until starting to colour, add the herbs and cook for another minute.

Remove to an oven proof casserole with lid. Cut the beef into 25mm cubes and brown all over in the same pan in which you cooked the onions. Do this in small batches if necessary. When all the meat has nicely coloured stir in the mustard and half the capers.

Add the meat to the casserole dish with the onions, ensuring all the crusty bits are incorporated, and return to the heat.

Add the cider and allow it to boil for about two minutes. Season well and add a bay leaf. Put the lid on and cook in the oven at 180°C for one hour. Depending on the tenderness of the meat at this stage, add the pearl barley.

For the next 40 minutes continue cooking on the stove top over a low heat with the lid off. Stir occasionally to prevent sticking and top up with water as the barley thickens the stew. The dish is ready when the meat is tender and the liquid has thickened and reduced. Just before serving add the remaining capers.

Like all slow cooked stews this is even better cooked the day before and also freezes well.

VEAL ESCALOPE WITH CARAMELISED APPLES AND A SIMPLE CIDER SAUCE

Annabelle Jackman, West Milton Cider Club

This very tasty recipe goes equally well with veal or pork chops.
It is easy to prepare and looks very impressive on the plate.
A great one for a last minute supper with unexpected guests.

4 veal escalopes about 150g each
1 small onion finely chopped.
1 stick of celery finely chopped
50g butter
1 tbsp oil
200ml medium cider
100ml double cream
lemon juice to taste (optional)
2 crisp eating apples
salt and pepper

Serves 4

Dry the escalopes with kitchen paper and slightly flatten. Season with salt and pepper.
Heat a frying pan with oil and 25g of butter. Add the veal.
Peel and core the apples and cut them into eight lengthways.
Heat the remaining butter in another pan until hot. Add the apple pieces. Cook on a high heat to brown and caramelise the outside whilst the inside retains a bit of crunch. This should not take more than about five minutes for both sides. Remove from the pan and set aside to keep warm. Any butter left in the pan can be added to the meat.
As the escalopes near the end of cooking, after about eight to ten minutes depending on the thickness, add the chopped onion and celery. When the meat is cooked remove but keep warm. Now add the cider and allow to bubble away quite fast so that the vegetables cook and the liquid reduces by half.
Add the cream and stir everything together as it cooks for another two minutes. Adjust the seasoning and add a small amount of lemon juice to slightly sharpen the flavour.
To serve, place each escalope on a plate with four segments of apple on top. Spoon the sauce around the veal and serve immediately.

ROAST LAMB WITH ASTURIAN CIDER

Arthur Watson, Riverside Restaurant, West Bay

This roast lamb with Spanish cider from Asturias and delicious apples is the perfect Spanish lamb dish. The slow cooking allows all the flavours to infuse and create a fantastic gravy.

1 leg of lamb about 2½kg
5 garlic cloves skins left on and halved or roughly squashed
4 apples cored and quartered
500ml asturian cider or an artisan cider
olive oil
few sprigs of thyme or rosemary
juice of half a lemon
salt and pepper
500ml chicken or lamb stock

Serves 8

Preheat the oven to high, then score the lamb in a criss-cross pattern, drizzle with a little olive oil and rub in salt and pepper.
Place the lamb in a deep roasting tin and add the garlic and herbs, pour over the lemon juice, add an extra drizzle of olive oil and cook in the hot oven.
After 30 minutes, turn the heat right down. Place the apples into the tin and pour in the cider and return to the oven for a couple of hours. When the lamb is cooked, remove from the tin and place onto a cutting board, cover with foil and leave to rest while you prepare the sauce.
Place a sieve over a pan and tip in the contents of the roasting tin (everything will be nice and soft), squashing down so you get out the juices. Discard the pulp remaining and add the stock to the pan with the juices, boil until the sauce is the thickness you like.
Serve with the sauce and fresh greens and potatoes for a warming, fruity and succulent dinner.

SMOKED GAMMON WITH CIDER

Liz Copas, National Association of Cider Makers'
Orcharding Advisor and Field Trial Officer

4 thick slices of smoked gammon
300ml cider
bouquet garni
peppercorns
1 tbsp cider vinegar
50g butter

Put the slices of gammon in a shallow casserole
and cover with cider.
Add peppercorns and a bouquet garni.
Bring to the boil and simmer for 30 minutes.
Drain the slices of gammon and then fry them in
butter. Brown both sides turning frequently.
Remove the gammon and keep warm.
Deglaze the pan with the vinegar and pour the
sauce over the gammon.

Serves 4

CIDER AND LENTIL PILAF

Mark and Sue Johnson, Eggardon Kitchen, Nettlecombe

1 onion chopped finely
1 green pepper deseeded and
finely chopped
1 carrot peeled and finely chopped
2 sticks of celery finely chopped
4 cloves of garlic finely chopped
1 small green chilli chopped
½ tsp each of coriander, cumin,
turmeric, and cayenne pepper
150g puy lentils
250ml cider
1 tbsp olive oil
salt & black pepper
fresh coriander roughly chopped

In a large pan heat the oil. Add onion and slowly sweat until soft.
Add the garlic and spices.
Now add the rest of the chopped vegetables and cook them slowly for a couple of minutes.
Add lentils and cider.
Cook until the lentils are just soft.
Season to taste
Serve with rice or bulgar wheat and fresh coriander.

Serves 3-4

CREAMY CYDERY GREEN BEANS WITH LEEKS

Torkard Ray & Gail, The Marches Cyder Circle

These piquant creamy cydery green beans with leeks
can be served up with most white meats or grilled sausages,
or alongside other vegetables such as roasted peppers for a meat-free meal.

400 - 500g green beans (runner or
  French)
500ml dry 100% juice real cyder
  (not all of this will be required)
2 leeks washed, trimmed and
finely sliced
100g mushrooms: wiped and
  finely sliced
150ml pot soured cream
oil for frying
freshly ground black pepper
salt to taste

After washing, trimming and slicing the green beans, tip them into a hot oily wok or heavy-based frying pan, and stir to coat them in the hot oil.

After a couple of minutes of stir frying, add a good splash of dry cyder to the hot wok followed by the finely sliced leeks and then a splash more cyder. As the cyder evaporates, more is added to prevent any of the vegetables browning, the vegetables cooking through the steam of the cyder rather than actually frying in oil. After a couple of minutes add a few finely sliced mushrooms and then a little more cyder. Keep stirring and reduce the heat slightly.

When the vegetables are cooked through but still have a little bite, add the contents of a small pot of soured cream along with freshly ground black pepper and salt to taste. If required more cyder can be added.

Serves 2-4

CIDER SYLLABUB

Maya Pieris, Four Seasons Preserves, Askerswell

Serve with the cider drizzle cake or with brandy snaps or ginger biscuits.
Also good as a trifle topping or with meringue and apple puree for a 'Bridport Mess'!

150ml double cream
20g icing sugar
grated nutmeg
1 tsp lemon juice
1 tsp grated lemon rind
100ml dry cider

Whisk the double cream until it begins to thicken.
Add icing sugar, grated nutmeg to your taste or another sweet spice, lemon juice and grated lemon rind. Slowly add the dry cider making sure it mixes in.

Serves 4

CIDER SYLLABUB AND/OR CHEESECAKE

Penny Whatmoor, Owermoigne Cider Museum

100ml dry cider
120g caster sugar
3 tbsp cider brandy
zest and juice of a lemon
280ml chilled double cream

Mix sugar, cider, brandy and lemon zest together in a medium bowl.
Add lemon juice and mix again.
Gradually whisk in cream until it forms soft peaks.
Spoon into glasses.
Serve with slices of fresh apple.

For a cider cheesecake substitute half the cream for cream cheese and spoon onto a base of crushed digestive biscuits and melted butter. Chill for an hour.

Serves 4

CIDER SURPRISE

Andrew Whittle, Nettlecombe Cider Club, Nettlecombe

A great way to use up some of that cider that is just the wrong side of drinkable.

3 apples
2 bananas
some grapes
caster sugar
1 pint of cider
cinnamon
nutmeg
cardamom

Serves 4

Peel and cut the fruit into bite size chunks, place in a bowl and dust with sugar.
In a separate bowl put cider and add the spices to taste.
Allow the cider to stand, this is important
Finally pour the cider down the sink and eat the fruit with yoghurt or cream

PEARS AND CIDER JELLY

Margaret Morgan-Grenville, West Milton Cider Club

6 pears
500ml real cider
100g sugar
½ lemon
½ orange
a mulling bag
sachet of powdered gelatine

Serves 6

Mull the cider, sugar, lemon and orange juice for five minutes.
Add six pears peeled and quartered to the liquid and poach for about 20 minutes.
Take out the pears and strain the juice. Measure the juice and use enough gelatine to set the amount - about a sachet.
Put three tablespoons of juice in a small bowl and sprinkle powdered gelatine on top. After five minutes, put the bowl in a pan of barely simmering water until the gelatine has liquefied. It's worth straining to remove any bits of skin. Add to the remaining juice and refrigerate in a jelly mould or in individual bowls.
Serve jelly and pears along with a good vanilla ice cream.
It looks rather dull but you will surprise all your guests as the taste is sensational.

CREPES SUCREES WITH APPLES & CALVADOS

Annabelle Jackman, West Milton Cider Club

For the crêpes

Makes 12 small or 6 large ones

125g plain flour
30g sugar
A pinch of salt
300ml full milk
100ml water
1 medium egg and 1 egg yolk
30g melted butter
unsalted butter for frying

For the apples

4 apples e.g. Golden Delicious
90g unsalted butter
4 tbsp caster sugar
180ml calvados or cider brandy

crème fraiche or vanilla ice-cream
to serve
Icing sugar for dusting

Serves 6

Make the pancake batter and let it rest.
Peel, core and quarter the apples and cut them into slices, three to four millimetres thick.
Melt the butter and once it is bubbling, add the apples. Cook over a medium heat, turning the slices to coat them in butter, and then add the sugar so that the outsides caramelise. The apples should be golden and soft but not floppy. Add the cider brandy and set aside.
To cook the pancakes, heat a very small amount of unsalted butter in the pan and add some of the batter. These crêpes need to be thin, so as soon as the batter hits the heat of the pan, quickly swirl it around and pour off any excess. Cook over a medium heat until golden and set underneath, flip it over, and cook the other side. To serve everyone at once, keep the cooked crêpes in a pile in a low oven. Fill each pancake with apple, add a blob of crème fraîche or ice-cream and, if you wish, fold the pancake over and sift with a little icing sugar to finish.

CIDER BAKED APPLES WITH A MAIZE CRUST

Lesley Waters

Serve this mulled pie with thick Dorset cream or vanilla ice-cream.

For the pastry

140g plain flour
55g instant dried polenta or
  semolina
pinch salt
115g butter
1 large egg, beaten
cold water

For the filling

6 large dessert apples, peeled,
  cored and halved
55g unsalted butter, melted
150ml fruity cider
25g soft brown sugar
sprig rosemary
caster sugar for sprinkling

Serves 6-8

Preheat the oven to 200°C.

Into a large bowl, sieve the flour, salt and polenta. Rub in the butter until the mixture resembles fine breadcrumbs. Stir in the egg and enough water to bind the dough together. Chill the pastry for 30 minutes.

Place the apples in a shallow, round oven proof dish approx. 23cm in diameter. Combine the melted butter with the cider and pour over the apples. Sprinkle the apples with the brown sugar and tuck in the sprig of rosemary.

On a lightly floured surface, roll out the pastry until it is large enough to lay as a blanket over the apples. Carefully lift the pastry over the apples and roughly trim the edges and tuck inside the dish. Lightly sprinkle the pastry with the caster sugar.

Bake the pie for 10 minutes, then reduce the oven to 170°C. Bake for a further 30-35 minutes until the apples are softened and cooked.

VANILLA ICE CREAM

4 egg yolks
100g caster sugar
300ml milk
300ml double cream
1 vanilla pod, split

Makes 1½ pints

Put the milk and vanilla pod in a saucepan and over a low heat bring to the boil.

In a bowl, beat the egg yolks and sugar together and then still beating, pour in the milk and vanilla pod.

Return the custard to the pan and stir constantly over a low heat until the custard forms a film over the back of a wooden spoon. Do not allow the custard to boil or it will separate.

Remove the pan from the heat. Allow the custard to cool and stir in the cream.

Transfer to an ice-cream maker and follow the manufacturer's instructions.

MULLED PEARS & FRANGIPANE TART WITH CIDER CREAM

Nick Poole, West Milton Cider Company

A great marriage of flavour between the pears, almond and mulled cider cream. It is a good one to prepare in advance and glaze it just before serving to give it that extra sparkle.

3 ripe but firm pears, peeled and
  halved lengthways
500ml medium or sweet cider
sachet of mulling spices, or
1 tsp cinnamon, ½ tsp allspice,
½ tsp ground ginger, pinch of
  nutmeg and a whole clove
  wrapped in a piece of muslin.
30g sugar.
100ml of double cream

For the frangipane
150g butter at room temperature
150g icing sugar or castor sugar
150g of ground almonds
2 eggs
few drops of almond essence
2 tbsp apricot jam

Serves 6

Add the spices and sugar to the cider in a saucepan, place the pears, in one layer and simmer gently until the pears are tender but not too soft. When cooked remove and allow to cool and drain, they need to be quite dry.

Meanwhile make the frangipane. Beat the butter and sugar until pale and creamy (about three minutes) with an electric whisk. Beat the eggs in a separate bowl and add a little at a time to the mix, adding a small quantity of the ground almonds after each addition. Finish off by adding the remaining almond and essence then spread the mixture into the base of a 20cm loose-based flan ring.

Now slice the cooled pears across into about seven or eight slices, slightly flatten each half and place on the frangipane in a cartwheel style. Bake in an oven at 180˚C for about 25 minutes, or until the tart is firm and nicely browned on top. The pears will have sunk slightly into the mixture.

While it is cooling heat the apricot jam in a small pan, adding a small drop of water or cider to loosen it. Pour this mixture through a strainer and glaze just the pears.

To make the cider cream, boil the remaining mulled cider until it has reduced and started to become syrupy. Measure out 50ml and simply add it to the cream. This is equally good served warm or cold with the tart, which is best eaten at room temperature.

ZABAGLIONE

Hugh Fearnley-Whittingstall

This is my version of zabaglione: the heady but light-as-air Italian dessert. It does take a bit of whisking – an electric whisk is essential, unless you have the arms of Hercules – but it uses only three storecupboard ingredients to produce something very delicious and elegant. I'm assuming your storecupboard includes a bottle of brandy, as mine does – Somerset cider brandy lends a special flavour here. Rich and creamy (although actually dairy-free), this pud is lovely served alone, or with a fairly plain little biscuit, such as a langue de chat or savoiarde, for dipping. It's also stunningly good heaped over raspberries.

8 large egg yolks
75g caster sugar
100ml cider brandy

Serves 6

Pour a four to five centimetre depth of water into a large saucepan and set it to simmer on the hob.

Put the egg yolks and sugar in a large heatproof bowl and whisk together with an electric whisk for two to three minutes, until thick and creamy. Stand the bowl over the pan of gently simmering water and slowly whisk in the brandy. Continue whisking until the mixture is pale, thick and billowy, and roughly quadrupled in volume. If you lift the beaters, the 'trail' that falls on to the mixture should hold its shape for a few seconds, before slowly sinking back in. This will take at least 10, more likely 15 or 20 minutes, so you might want to make sure you have a glass of wine, or a cup of tea at the very least, by your elbow. Ensure that the water in the pan is only just simmering and that the bowl doesn't get too hot, or the eggs will start to cook and the mixture may split.

Serve straight away or at least within minutes, while still warm, in elegant glasses. After 20 – 30 minutes, it will start to separate.

CIDER DRIZZLE CAKE

Maya Pieris, Four Seasons Preserves, Askerswell

Cake

3 eggs
their weight in self-raising flour,
  soft brown or caster sugar and
  soft margarine or butter
1 tsp cinnamon
2 medium eating apples

Cider Syrup

100ml dry cider
50ml apple juice
1 tsp lemon juice
20g brown sugar
1 tsp ground ginger

Weigh three eggs and then their weight in self-raising flour, sugar (soft brown or caster if preferred) and soft margarine or soft butter. Add cinnamon.

Mix for a minute or so with a hand whisk till smooth.

Peel, core and chop the apples into small pieces and stir into the cake mix.

Pour into a greased and lined loaf tin, a one 'lb' tin or a 17cm round or square tin.

Bake for about 30 - 40 minutes at 180°C until an inserted skewer comes out clean.

Leave to cool in the tin.

Gently heat dry cider, apple juice, lemon juice, brown sugar and ground ginger until the sugar is dissolved. Then turn up the heat until slightly reduced – sorry if that is a bit vague but you want the liquid to be syrupy! Pour over the cooled cake and leave in the tin overnight in the fridge to settle. Be careful when you turn out the cake as it will be quite soft.

Serve with cream, yoghurt, crème fraiche or cider syllabub.

Illustrated on p.63 - middle right

OXFORDSHIRE CYDER APPLE CAKE

Sandie & Oxford Tom, The Marches Cyder Circle

225g butter
350g self raising flour
1½ tsp ground cinnamon
120g of sultanas (or raisins)
  soaked for an hour or two
  in 50ml dry cyder
175g caster sugar
400g mixed eating and cooking
apples
3 large eggs
demerara sugar (for dusting the
  top of the cake after it is cooked)

Preheat the oven to 180°C. Grease and line a 20 cm loose-bottomed cake tin.
Mix flour, cinnamon and butter until it resembles breadcrumbs (a food processor on 'pulse' works well).
Stir in the sugar, and sultanas and cyder.
Peel, core and roughly chop the apples and add to the mixture.
Beat eggs lightly and stir into the mixture.
Spoon mixture into the cake tin and bake for 60 - 75 minutes, or until cooked (check with a skewer, until it comes away 'clean').
While it is hot sift over the demerara sugar and leave in the tin on a cooling rack until thoroughly cool.
Enjoy with a glass of cyder!

CYMRU CYDER CAKE

Upland Phill, The Marches Cyder Circle

330ml sweet 100% juice real cyder
300g plain flour
2 tsp bicarbonate of soda
1 tsp mixed spice powder
1 tsp ground cinnamon
pinch freshly grated nutmeg
4 cox's (or alternate good sharp
  British type) apples, peeled, cored
  and grated
150g soft dark brown sugar
150g melted butter
2 free range eggs
200g golden sultanas
100g pecans, chopped

Preheat the oven to 180°C.

Place the cyder into a pan over a high heat. Bring to the boil and cook until reduced by two-thirds.

Sift the plain flour, bicarbonate of soda, mixed spice powder, cinnamon and nutmeg into a bowl.

In a separate bowl, mix the apples with the sugar and butter.

Add the eggs and reduced cyder to the apple mixture and stir well.

Add the spiced flour mixture to the apple mixture and mix well.

Add the sultanas and pecans and fold together to combine.

Spoon the cake mixture into a 20 centimetre spring-form cake tin and bake in the oven for 45 - 60 minutes, or until a skewer comes out clean when pushed into the centre of the cake. Turn out the cake onto a wire rack and leave to cool.

For an extra kick try adding a shot or two of calvados to the reduced cyder.

Great with a cuppa when picking in an orchard.

Illustrated opposite - on the left

EGGARDON CIDER APPLE CAKE

Mark and Sue Johnson, Eggardon Kitchen, Nettlecombe

Cake
675g cooking apples
225g self-raising flour
100g butter
100g golden caster sugar
2 eggs
100ml cider

Topping
100g golden granulated sugar
75g butter
100g self-raising flour

Preheat the oven to 180°C.
Make the topping first by mixing all the ingredients together - you are looking for the texture of breadcrumbs.
Cream butter and sugar together.
Add the eggs.
Fold in the flour.
Add cider until you have a dropping consistency.
Put in a 20cm greased round loose bottom cake tin.
Peel and slice apples and scatter on top of the mixture in the tin.
Cover with topping and lightly press down.
Bake in the oven for 60 - 90 minutes.
Leave to cool in tin for 10 minutes.
Serve warm with clotted cream.

Illustrated below and on p.63

PUFF PASTRY WITH CIDER

Marie-Anne & Michel Ameline, Normandy

250ml cider (medium)
200g salted butter
300g flour
2 tbsp brown sugar

Put the cider and butter in a big saucepan. Bring to the boil.
When the butter has melted turn off the gas and add the flour and sugar all at once.
Mix it quickly together with a wooden spoon.
Put pastry into a bowl and allow to cool at room temperature.
Leave it a few hours or overnight in the fridge well wrapped.
Take it out of the fridge 30 minutes before using.
Roll it out quite thinly.
It will keep for a week in the fridge and it freezes well.

Enough for 2 tarts

Don't add the sugar If needed for a savoury dish.

CIDER PANCAKES

Marie-Anne & Michel Ameline, Normandy

250g flour
250ml sweet cider
250ml milk
(or 500 ml cider instead)
3 eggs
vanilla extract
pinch of salt

optional
3 tbsp cider brandy
grated rind of lemon or orange

Put flour and salt in a basin. Add eggs and mix gradually adding cider and milk. Beat well.
Add the melted butter and vanilla.
Add grated rind and cider brandy if you like.
Leave to rest for 30 minutes to an hour (optional).
Heat pan and cook the pancakes.

CIDER BREAD

Martin Inwood, Lulworth Skipper, Wareham

500g good quality strong bread flour
750ml real dry cider
2 tsps sugar
pinch of salt
7g sachet of dried yeast
(about 1½ tsp)

Pour two-thirds of the cider into a stainless steel pan and simmer to drive off the alcohol. A shame, I know, but the yeast will not get on with alcohol.

Dissolve two teaspoons of sugar in the cider.

Cool to blood temperature and add yeast. Cover and put in a warm place.

The surplus cider in the glass is for you to enjoy while you are baking!

Add salt to the flour in a large mixing bowl.

When the cider and yeast starter is in full swing, form a well in the middle of the flour and using a steel spoon or your hands bring it all together into a ball of dough. If the mixture is too dry add a drop of warm water. Turn the dough out and knead for 10 minutes, until you have a nice stretchy, springy dough.

Return the dough to a clean, oiled bowl, cover in cling film and put it in a warm place to prove (double in size) for about 45 minutes.

Turn out the dough, 'knock it back' and knead for a minute reducing size. Shape into a loaf to suit your tin, I use the lid of a poultry roaster so its a rugby ball shape for me.

Cover with a clean tea towel and leave to prove for 30 minutes.

Preheat your oven to 200°C.

Slash the top with a sharp knife and dust with flour. Bake for 15 minutes at 200°C then reduce the heat to 190°C for a further 35 minutes: this will allow a very nice crust to form.

When fully baked your loaf should give a hollow ring when struck on the bottom.

Cool on a wire rack.

DORSET FONDUE

Julia and Ken Hendrickson, West Milton Cider Club

*Why go to Switzerland when you can do just as well with this
scrumptious dish from the West Milton Cider Club*

½ small onion
250ml dry cider
1 tsp lemon juice
375g grated cheddar cheese
½ tsp dry mustard
3 tsp cornflour
3 tbsp apple juice
pinch of white pepper

*wedges of apple and cubes of
crusty bread, to serve*

Serves 4-6

Rub the inside of the fondue pot with cut side of onion.
Pour in the cider and lemon juice and heat gently until bubbling. Reduce the heat to low and gradually stir in the grated cheese, then continue to heat until the cheese melts, stirring frequently.
In a small bowl, blend mustard and cornflour smoothly with apple juice. Stir into the cheese mixture and continue to cook for two to three minutes until the mixture is thick and creamy, stirring frequently. Season with pepper.
Serve with wedges of apple and cubes of crusty bread.

MOLLIE RENDELL'S APPLE CHUTNEY

Matthew Bryant, Haselbury Plucknett

My grandmother's recipe from Haselbury Plucknett.
This is excellent when made with surplus cider apples.

450g of onions
250ml of spiced vinegar
splash of cider
900g of apples (after chopping and
  peeling)
125g sultanas
1 tsp salt
1 tsp ground ginger
375g sugar

Peel and finely chop onions and put into saucepan with the vinegar and simmer until nearly soft.

Chop apples and add to pan, with sultanas, salt, ground ginger and just enough vinegar to stop mixture from burning.

Cook gently, stirring from time to time until the fruit is soft.

Add the rest of the vinegar and cider and thoroughly stir in the sugar. Bring to the boil and boil steadily until the chutney is thick.

Pour the chutney into clean, warm jars and seal.

APRICOT AND GINGER CIDER SAUCE

Oliver and Penny Strong, Dorset Nectar, Waytown

Delicious over baked chicken or potatoes

1 small onion – finely chopped
A small chilli (optional)
300ml chicken or vegetable stock
300ml cider
200g plump dried apricots,
  finely chopped
3cm of fresh ginger root
  finely chopped
4 tbsp cornflour to thicken

Sauté the onion until golden in oil or coconut butter. A small chilli can be added according to taste.
Add the chopped apricots and fresh ginger root and continue cooking for a few minutes.
Add the cider and chicken or vegetable stock and bring to a simmer.
Combine the cornflour or flour with half a cup of water. Take the saucepan off the heat and stir in the thickener. Continue stirring until the sauce starts to thicken, then simmer for five minutes on a very low heat.
The sauce can be blended until smooth.

Serves 6

MARCLE RIDGE BROWN PLUM SAUCE

Nigel & Debs, The Marches Cyder Circle

*Enjoy with egg and chips or cheese sarnies
accompanied by a pint of 100% juice real cyder!*

1kg plums or 1.8kg damsons
3 medium onions
100g sultanas
15g root ginger
25g pickling spice
950ml malt vinegar (or substitute
  cyder/perry vinegar!)
225g granulated sugar
50g salt
25g dry mustard
1 level tsp turmeric

Wipe and stone plums and put in a large pan. Don't worry if stones are stuck they'll come out later. Add onions & sultanas.

Bruise ginger (hit with a hammer). Tie in muslin along with pickling spice and add to the pan.

Add half the vinegar and boil for 30 minutes. Meanwhile warm sugar in very cool oven 110°C. Put clean jars in to sterilise at the same time. Remove the spice bag and stir in all the other ingredients.

Stir to dissolve the sugar and bring to boiling point.

Simmer for 40 - 60 minutes, stirring occasionally, then leave to cool.

When cool push the contents of the pan through a nylon sieve and remember to scrape the purée off the underside of the sieve

If too thin, simmer and reduce volume until desired consistency is reached.

Fill jars to brim, put on clean lids immediately and label, then store

Leave to mature for at least 4 weeks.

APPLE CIDER VINEGAR

Oliver and Penny Strong, Dorset Nectar

Unfiltered natural apple cider vinegar has been hailed through the ages as the elixir of life. There is written evidence of its use as an aid to good health from as long as 3000 BC in Egypt.

This nutritionally rich vinegar is a living food rich in enzymes and good bacterial microbes necessary for human digestion. It is not to be confused with the clear and refined apple cider vinegar sold in the grocery stores.

Natural apple cider vinegar is made from whole crushed organically grown cider apples. It is unfiltered and contains a web-like, cloudy substance called the 'mother', formed from naturally occurring pectin and apple residues. This natural vinegar is full of live enzymes and minerals such as potassium and is used to aid a myriad of aliments from arthritis to normalising blood sugars in diabetes.

It is specifically these qualities that make this kind of unpasteurised traditional vinegar sought after by the health food and alternative medicine market.

Today there is scientific evidence that the high phenolic content of cider apples particularly helps in reducing arterial plaque and reducing the chances of suffering a heart attack or stroke.

There is also recent scientific evidence that vinegar has marked antiglycemic properties and could be very helpful to those suffering from diabetes.

The most exciting medicinal use of apple cider vinegar recently is in the fight against arthritis, as it has been found that a regimen of apple cider vinegar and honey breaks down the calcium deposits in the joints, while re-mineralising the bones, so helping to alleviate the pain caused by this condition.

Natural apple cider vinegar has been used as an aid to digestion as the natural biological activity produces enzymes that break down food into usable compounds'.

It has also, for millennia, been valued for its cleansing and detoxifying properties, breaking down the mucous and phlegm deposits in the body and so easing the effects of colds.

PRACTICAL VINEGAR TIPS

If you're short of an egg in your recipe while baking, 1 tablespoon of apple cider vinegar will compensate for the lack of an egg.

HEALTH TIPS

To minimise the misery of a cold
1 teaspoon of apple cider vinegar in a ¼ glass of water taken 3 times daily reduces the mucus and minimises the misery of having a cold.

For a Sore Throat
1 tablespoon of apple cider vinegar and a teaspoon of honey will give you a happy throat.

The enzymes and healthy bacteria in apple cider vinegar encourage healthy function of the digestive system

COCKTAILS

Nick Poole, West Milton Cider Company

Ante's extension

1m cider brandy
½m triple sec
1 red vermouth
½m double cream
1m cranberry juice

Shake on ice, serve in a
cocktail glass or tumbler

Apple Swizzle

2m cider brandy
½m white rum
1m lime juice
3 dashes angostura bitters
1 tsp sugar syrup

Shake with ice, serve in
a tumbler or add 3m of
Appletiser and serve in a
highball glass

Apples and Cherries or The Pink Lady's Cherry

1m cider brandy
1m cherry brandy
½m cream
½m lime juice

Shake and serve in a tumbler

Note: m = measure

GREEN MAN MULLED CYDER

Chateau Sharon, The Marches Cyder Circle

4½ litres of cyder
300ml water
peel of 1 orange
2 cinnamon sticks
6 whole cloves
½ tsp allspice
Sugar to taste

Place the orange peel, cinnamon sticks, cloves and allspice into a saucepan with the water and bring to the boil. Lower temperature and simmer for 30 minutes. Strain the liquid into a bowl, and put the strained spices into a muslin bag.
Add both of these to the cyder and slowly warm up in a large saucepan. Add sugar to taste. It is best to let the cyder mull for at least 30 - 45 minutes before drinking. Remove spice bag before serving in pre-warmed glasses or mugs. Do not boil as you will lose all the alcohol!

MULLED CIDER

Nigel Stewart, Bridge Farm, East Chinnock

4½ litres of cider
1½ cups brown sugar
½ tsp ginger
1½ tsp cloves
1½ tsp allspice
1½ sticks of cinnamon
½ tsp nutmeg
½ tsp salt

Place the sugar, spices, cider and salt into the saucepan. Heat and simmer for 20 minutes. Strain through muslin or a fine nylon strainer and rinse out the saucepan. Then return the strained liquor to the pan and reheat until piping hot (avoid boiling).

CONTRIBUTORS

Bridge Farm Cider. Nigel Stewart has been making artisan cider at Bridge farm, near Yeovil, since 1986. The apples are pressed using traditional rack and cloth methods with a hydraulic press dating from the early 1900s. Bridge Farm offers a large range of cider and apple juice in traditional dry, medium or sweet, also single varieties and pear cider. www.bridgefarmcider.co.uk

Burrow Hill Cider. Julian Temperley has long been known for his success in making cider at Kingsbury Episcopi in the Somerset Levels. In recent years he has also greatly expanded his production of cider brandy and is now able to offer everything from three-year-old to 20-year-old bottles. His morello cherries marinated in cider brandy are a must for any dinner party. www.ciderbrandy.co.uk

Dorset Nectar. Dorset Nectar is an organic cider orchard and farm near Bridport, producing award winning traditional ciders from 11 varieties of cider apple, including Dabinets, Chisel Jerseys, Sweet Coppin and Porters Perfection. The artisan cider is made from naturally fermented juice using wild yeasts and no sulphites to create a delicious cider that is fruity and full of flavour. Dorset Nectar also produces nutritionally rich 'live enzyme vinegar' which is akin to a 'live' food. www.dorsetnectar.co.uk

Eggardon Kitchen. Long time members of the Powerstock community, Mark and Sue Johnson use their fantastic cooking skills to run an outside catering business from their kitchen at Browns Farm, Nettlecombe. During the summer months they also run the very popular Saw Mill Café at Mapperton House, near Beaminster. www.eggardonkitchen.co.uk

Highway Farm, Bridport. Accommodation and good food are always available from hosts Pauline and John Bale at their popular B&B establishment on the outskirts of Bridport, with arts and crafts courses to tempt you to visit. www.highwayfarm.co.uk

Hugh Fearnley-Whittingstall. Master chef and TV personality Hugh Fearnley-Whittingstall first moved to Dorset to create his River Cottage TV series for Channel 4 and included a visit to Powerstock Cider Festival in one of the programmes. He has now moved to East Devon near Axminster, where he continues to champion real food and creative cooking. www.rivercottage.net

Lesley Waters. Lesley is well known for her regular television appearances on *Ready Steady Cook*, *Great Food Live* and *This Morning*. She is also a former head tutor of Leiths' School of Food and Wine and author of several cookbooks. She now runs her own cookery school at Abbots Hill in Dorset and is regularly seen demonstrating her skills for quirky rustic style dishes at local food events and festivals. For details of her courses contact:
www.lesleywaters.com or ring 0844 800 4633.

Lulworth Skipper. Made by Martin Inwood, a small producer of award winning craft cider located in Purbeck. Local cider apples are pressed on a restored traditional oak twin screw press. Tastings by appointment and off sales from the cider shed. There is also an online shop. www.lulworth-skipper.com

Liz Copas. Liz spent twenty years as a leading pomologist at the Long Ashton Research Station. She is widely recognised in the cider world for her work in developing new cider apple varieties and for her highly acclaimed book *A Somerset Pomona*. She is also a member of the Society of Botanical Artists and has contributed several of her drawings to this book. www.lizcopas.com

Marquis of Lorne, Nettlecombe. This 16th century Inn at Nettlecombe is featured in many food and pub guides. Steve Brady is both the landlord and head chef, producing a varied and interesting menu to entertain his many happy diners. www.marquisoflorne.co.uk

Maya Pieris. Maya is a local food writer who also runs the award winning *Four Seasons Preserves*. "Moving to Dorset has been a move to food heaven and cider has been one of the local revelations," she says. www.four-seasons-preserves.co.uk

Mill House Cider Museum, Owermoigne. Don't miss the excellent display of historical cider making equipment on display here. The Museum also hosts cider-making days during the autumn and sells many different ciders from their shop. www.millhousecider.com

Marie-Anne & Michel Ameline and The Big Ben Restaurant, Fecamps, Normandy, France. Michel's enthusiasm for our Powerstock Cider Festival is second to none. Award-winning maker of *cidre bouché,* it is Marie-Anne's recipes with cider and links to their local restaurant on the quay at Fecamps that have given us a European contribution to this book.

Marches Cyder Circle. This friendly group of enthusiastic cyder makers and drinkers from in and around Herefordshire and the Welsh Marches like to keep it traditional with their excellent ciders and old-world spelling. Every year they make a great contribution to the Powerstock Festival - not just with their cyder but their fine singing voices, too.

Matthew Bryant. Matthew is a very enthusiastic amateur cider maker from Haselbury Plucknett, where he makes his cider and helps organise the local community orchard project. He also hosts the annual South Somerset Cider Sampling night at Hinton St George.

Nettlecombe Cider Club. Situated at the other end of Powerstock parish, the Nettlecombe club still make their cider in the traditional way on the old twin-screw press that once made cider for the entire Mappercombe Manor estate belonging to the Crutchley family. Victor Crutchley was keen to see the old equipment brought back to life and has since begun planting new orchards on the estate.

Riverside Restaurant, West Bay. This highly acclaimed seafood restaurant has been a gourmet's focal point at West Bay for many years. Under the guidance of owner Arthur Watson, it has won many awards and accolades and continues to be a magnet for food lovers from far and wide. www.thefishrestaurant-westbay.co.uk

The Ropemakers, Bridport. This is a busy town centre pub with a relaxed and friendly atmosphere. They serve traditional pub food made with the best local ingredients and also actively promote local music talent.
www.theropemakers.com

Roger's Cider. Mark Rogers of Twinways Orchard at Melplash, near Bridport, makes his traditional farmhouse ciders with a traditional oak screw press He is also kept busy with his large bee colony which complements the cider orchard and provides honey and honey based products for sale. Tel. 01308 488367

The Stable, The Bull, Bridport. Bridport's one-and-only full-time cider bar has been a great success since opening. Serving a wide range of ciders and providing highly comfortable hotel facilities in the heart of West Dorset. www.thebullhotel.co.uk

The Three Horseshoes, Powerstock. Landlord Carl Bashford is a great believer in real food and uses local sourced and foraged products to create some excellent dishes for his popular restaurant. His work is often experimental and he's not afraid of using the more unusual ingredients that other chefs sometimes overlook. www.thethreeshoesdorset.co.uk

West Milton Cider Club. Nick Poole started this local community project in 2000. The club has about twenty members who get together to make their cider in the autumn and then spend the rest of the year taking it home, or drinking it at their lunch meetings on the first Sunday of every month.

West Milton Cider Company. Offers both traditional draught cider and specialist bottle-conditioned ciders known as Lancombe Rising and West Dorset Fine Cider. All made from excellent quality local cider apples using 100% of the juice with no artificial flavourings or additives. This not only produces a great tasting cider. It is also excellent when used in cooking. www.westmiltoncider.co.uk

Worley's Cider. Neil Worley makes his traditional farmhouse cider in the Somerset village of Dean, near Shepton Mallet. He is very enthusiastic about his craft and after a small-scale start he is now expanding his business to keep up with the demand for his popular ciders. In between times he also helps judge cider classes at the Bath and West Show competition, and runs the South West of England Cider Makers Association website. www.worleyscider.co.uk

INDEX

CONVERSION TABLES

We have used metric measurements throughout the Cider Cookbook.
However you might find the following tables useful

OVEN TEMPERATURES

Gas	°C	°C Fan	°F	Temperature
¼	110	90	225	Very cool
½	120	100	250	Very cool
1	140	120	275	Cool or slow
2	150	130	300	Cool or slow
3	160	140	325	Warm
4	180	160	350	Moderate
5	190	170	375	Moderately hot
6	200	180	400	Fairly hot
7	220	200	425	Hot
8	230	210	450	Very hot
9	240	220	475	Very hot

MEASUREMENT EQUIVALENTS

Metric Grammes	Imperial Ounces	Metric Millilitres	Imperial Fluid Ounces
25	1	50	2
50	2	125	4
75	3	150	5 (¼ pint)
100	4 (¼ pound)	175	6
175	6	225	8
225	8 (½ pound)	300	10 (½ pint)
300	10	350	12
350	12 (¾ pound)	450	15 (¾ pint)
400	14	500	17
450	16 (1 pound)	600	20 (1 pint)

SPOON MEASURES

Use level spoon measures. As a guide:
1 teaspoon (tsp) = 5ml
1 tablespoon (tbsp) = 15ml